PASSING THE

Dominic Mc Ginley

ANNA
LIVIA

First published 1988 by
Borderline Publications
This Edition, 1990, Published by
Anna Livia Press
21 Cross Ave,
Dun Laoghaire,
Co. Dublin..

ISBN: 1 871311 05 5

AUTHOR'S ACKNOWLEDGEMENTS

My sincere thanks to my wife, Moya, for her unfailing encouragement throughout the preparation of this book. Thanks too for her typing and re-typing of the text.

Special thanks to Mr. Chris Heffernan who trained me in driving instruction; to Mr. Donal Moriarty, recently retired from the Driver Testing Section of the Department of the Environment; to Mr. G. Maher, Mr. B. Behan and Mr. J. Harte, also of Driver Testing, for giving so generously of their time. Thanks to Mr. Tony Herron for his encouragement. Sincere thanks to Garda Inspector P. O'Malley for his help regarding road traffic laws. Thanks also to Mr. David Lambe of Alexandra School of Motoring for his support. Special thanks to Mr. Tom Kerrigan and to Mr. Derek Farrell of the Disabled Drivers Association of Ireland for their help.

BIOGRAPHICAL NOTE

Dominic Mc Ginley was born in Dublin in 1954. He has trained as a Driving Instructor, and allied to this, he has a particular interest in text books and readability studies. Dominic is co-author and illustrator of a handbook published in 1987. He lives in Dublin's Northside and teaches in St. Colmcille's S.N.S., Donaghmede.

Cover Illustration by Ken Drakeford
Computer Graphics by John Maguire
Printed in Dublin by Colour Books Ltd.

CONTENTS

FOREWORD

This book is intended as a guide for learner drivers and driving test candidates. It is designed to help you as you prepare for your test. Knowing what to expect and what is expected of you while you are on test, should help you to pass your Driving Test.

This book is not about teaching yourself to drive and is not a substitute for good Driving Lessons.

Since the Rules of the Road are essential to good, safe motoring, I have made use of the present edition of this booklet in compiling the text. I have referred to the official forms and documents relating to Driver Licensing and also to the Road Traffic Acts and their amendments.

Many people remember that in 1979 there was an amnesty. Because of this thousands of people who held their second or third Provisional Driving Licence, were allowed to buy their Full Driving Licence without having to undergo the Driving Test. This was allowed by order of the then Minister for the Environment.

In spite of the hopes of current Provisional Licence holders such an amnesty will never be repeated. This is because of a European Commission directive issued in 1980.

Irish drivers pay dearly for motor insurance. Drivers who hold only a Provisional Licence pay much more than Full Licence holders. If a Full Licence means cheaper insurance, then why not do the Driving Test? And while you are at it, why not pass the test first time round?

According to the Department of the Environment 62,000 driving tests were carried out in 1987. Of the drivers tested 53% passed. This means that 29,140 people failed. So why did so many drivers fail?

Contrary to popular belief Driver Testers do not have a failure quota. The simple fact is that on the day of the test those drivers did not show themselves to be worthy of a Certificate of Competency.

The Driver Testers of the Department of the Environment are very experienced in their job. They are also highly trained. Your task is to show that you are capable of handling your vehicle with confidence and competence, with proper regard for your own safety and the safety of other road users, while putting the Rules of the Road into practice.

If you do this then you will pass the test. Many drivers approach the test as if they were bound to fail it the first time round. With a course of good instruction, plenty of practice, adequate preparation and a good knowledge of the Rules of the Road the Driving Test should not pose you any problem.

I hope that you will find this book useful.

Dominic McGinley

THE
LEARNER DRIVER

U ntil you have passed your Driving Test you are still a Learner Driver. This means that you must display "L" plates on the front and rear of your vehicle. "L" plates must be at least 15 cms high and be red on a white background. This does not apply to motorcycles or tractors.

You must hold a current Provisional Driving Licence for the category of vehicle you intend to drive. A Provisional Licence only entitles you to drive the category of vehicle listed on it.

During the period of your first, third and any subsequent Provisional Licence you must be accompanied by a fully qualified driver. This does not apply during the period of your second Provisional Licence. In this way you are encouraged to pass the test before your second Provisional Licence has expired.

Your vehicle must display a current Road Fund Tax Disc. It is an offence under the Road Traffic Act not to display a current disc.

Since 1986 motorists have been legally obliged to display a current insurance disc on their vehicles. If you drive a motor vehicle in any public place you must be covered by insurance. This is the law!

Motorcyclist Provisional Licence holders may not carry pillion passengers.

If, however, your vehicle is a W category tractor or a work-vehicle you may only carry a passenger if the vehicle can accommodate a passenger and your passenger has a full licence to drive that vehicle. The simple rule about licences and insurance is: *If in doubt, ask.*

All passenger vehicles with seating for not more than eight persons (excluding the driver) and goods vehicles which weigh not more than one and a half tons (unladen), registered on or after June 1st 1971, must have safety belts fitted. Statistics show that wearing a safety belt increases your chances of escaping injury or death in a road accident.

A heavy fine may be imposed on motorists who do not wear a seat belt while driving. You are responsible for ensuring that you are properly strapped in. You are also responsible for ensuring the safety of children travelling in the front passenger seat. If the child is younger than 12 and less than 150cms tall she or he should wear a proper safety restraint while travelling in the front passenger seat. Front seat passengers under 17 years of age must wear a safety belt and *you* must ensure this. Adult passengers in the front seat are themselves responsible for ensuring that they are securely strapped in.

LEARNER DRIVERS AND OTHER MOTORISTS

It seems that for many qualified motorists the red "L" plate of the learner driver is like a red rag to a bull. That little red "L"drives them berserk. They hoot their horns, roll their eyes, shake their fists, mutter under their breath and often do the most outrageous things to avoid the red menace. These fits of mania tend to be twice as bad if the learner driver is female. But don't worry, these fits pass! These motorists may even overtake on the wrong side of the road, risking death or serious injury, only to be delayed at the next set of traffic lights. You should never take this kind of behaviour seriously. It is not meant personally. These motorists have simply forgotten that they too once had "L" plates and were in the same position as you are now!

Learning any new skill can be very trying! This is particularly true of learning to drive. You may find that at times you are full of confidence and carry out every instruction perfectly. At other times you may feel you have forgotten everything you've been taught and that you should give up altogether. But don't despair. Learning to drive takes practice and if everyone was a perfect driver there would be no need for Driving Tests in the first place.

Learner Drivers generally need between 25 and 35 hours of motoring experience before they are ready to take the test. This is merely an estimate, as some learners will take less, others longer, to master the skills required to achieve a Certificate of Competency. It has been suggested that you should have a one-hour lesson for every year of your life, i.e. 18 hours for an eighteen-year old, etc.

Your driving experience should take account of all types of motoring situations. If you usually drive in country areas don't forget to get some city driving practice and vice versa. The forty seven Driver Testing Centres around the country are situated in towns or cities, so you will need to practise in built-up areas. If you are nervous of a particular type of traffic situation then that is where you need to gain experience. If you avoid the difficult situations you could be ensuring failure in the test.

So the message is: Practise! Practise! Practise!

3

SCHOOLS OF MOTORING

Most learner drivers prefer to go to a School of Motoring. There are a great many fine Schools of Motoring around the country. Some are large and have many branches, with an established reputation in the field of Driving Instruction. Some schools specialise in instruction on Heavy Goods Vehicles, i.e. trucks and articulated lorries or Public Service Vehicles such as buses. Others cater mainly for cars and a very few cater for motorcyclists.

Most learner drivers do not know what to expect when they approach a School of Motoring for the first time.

Here are some suggestions about what you might look for when seeking professional driving instruction. Even if you have decided to take lessons from a non-professional instructor, you will benefit greatly from some initial lessons in a Driving School car. You will have the comfort and security of knowing that the instructor has dual-pedal controls and you will become familiar with the idea of taking instruction.

If possible, follow the recommendation of others. If a particular instructor is recommended to you then ask for him or her. Confidence in your instructor is very important. After all, you are paying for the lessons.

Remember that all teachers have a different approach and method. The type of instruction given by a particular instructor may not suit your needs as a learner driver. If, after two or three lessons with a certain instructor, you are not happy with your progress then ask for a different instructor. Most Motoring Schools will be happy to oblige.

Consistency of instruction is most important, so try to arrange your lessons with the same instructor. He or she will be familiar with your progress and your particular difficulties in learning to drive. Large Motoring Schools may sometimes have slight problems in this area, as certain instructors may be in continuous demand, do make reasonable allowances for this!

It is worthwhile checking out the cost and duration of lessons. Some lessons last 45 minutes only, whereas others last an hour. This may vary around the country.

Some Motoring Schools expect you to go to them, while others will arrange to pick you up. Unless otherwise stated, you can take it that the pick-up time is included in the time of the lesson.

Some schools may allow you to share a lesson with a friend. This means that while you are under instruction your partner can benefit by observation and vice versa.

The 45-60 minute lesson is ideal for absolute beginners as tension is high and the lesson can seem like an eternity. But as you gain confidence double lessons may be more useful as you may find that you are just settling in to the lesson when it is over.

It makes sense to make notes about each lesson. Write down your strong and weak points. Build up a picture of your driving ability.

Many people find driving lessons embarrassing at first - after all, nobody likes to look foolish in front of others! Naturally, you want to do well and make as few mistakes as possible. This is where this book can help by giving you a good idea of what to expect.

Use the Table of Contents as a checklist of skills, procedures and manoeuvres to monitor your progress.

If there is a particular manoeuvre you have not been taught then you should ask!

Another suggestion is that you observe the driving of others, whether or not you are in a vehicle. But whatever you do don't become a back seat driver! It is *not* appropriate for you to comment - even if you are right!After all, you are still a learner driver and you will probably be told so!

You can learn a lot by observation. Think the manoeuvres through and mentally follow the correct procedure. Then when next you are behind the steering wheel you will be aware of what you should be doing.

THE TEST AND DRIVING
INSTRUCTION

Since the Road Traffic Act of 1968 the Government has had the right to regulate the giving of driving instruction for reward. However, no such regulations have ever been drawn up or implemented. This means that at present it is not necessary to have a special qualification to give driving lessons. Anyone with a full driving licence may give instruction on how to drive the same   categories   of vehicle which they are qualified to drive. Not everyone, though, is good at imparting information or knowledge.

It must be said, however, that many learner drivers successfully take the test after good and careful instruction from a friend or relation who is not a professional driving instructor. If you have confidence in your instructor there is no reason why you should not take instruction from a non-professional.

A word of caution, though. Do not to try to teach yourself! There are several good reasons for this advice. The first of these is that your lack of experience could prove fatal. It must be remembered that any motor vehicle can be a lethal weapon and your safety and the safety of others depends on your ability to handle your vehicle properly.

Since you are required by law to be accompanied by the holder of a Full Driving Licence, except during the period of your second Provisional Licence, why not benefit from his or her driving experience, even if you are also getting professional instruction. There is no shortcut to experience and everyone can benefit from advice.

Key elements of good driving instruction are:

- The ability to build a pupil's confidence, while putting them at ease.
- Patience.
- A thorough knowledge of the Rules of the Road and how to apply them.
- The ability to impart information in a helpful and non-antagonistic way.
- Coolness under pressure.
- The confidence to take control if the situation demands.
- The ability to demonstrate specific manoeuvres to driving test standard.

Perhaps the main reason for not taking instruction from a close friend or relation is that arguments can develop. This could prove to be dangerous if the argument were to arise at a critical moment in traffic, or indeed it could put a strain on the relationship. Only you can judge whether or not this kind of instruction will prove valuable.

There is no sense in putting a perfectly good friendship at risk for the sake of getting your driving licence, so you should seriously consider going to a reputable School of Motoring.

DRIVING LICENCES AND THE TEST

The new E.C. Model Driving Licences were introduced by the Minister for the Environment on November 13th 1989. This follows Directive 80/1263 from the E.C. The phasing out of the "old" licensing system will be completed by Nov. 13th 1992. As the main emphasis of this text is on motorcars and motorcycles details for other vehicles is necessarily brief.

A summary of the main features of the "new" system regarding all vehicles is available from your nearest vehicle licensing authority. The Road Traffic (Licensing of Drivers) Regulations, 1989 are available from the Government Publications Office and give more details again.

European Communities Model Licence Vehicle Categories
(Minimum Age of Driver in Brackets)

A1 Motorcycles under 125c.c., with or without sidecar [16]

A Motorcycles with or without sidecar [18] See Page 34

B Cars and light commercial vehicles with passenger accommodation for 8 persons or less, with design g.v.w. not over 3,500kg [17]

C1 Vehicles with Passenger accommodation for 8 persons or less, with design g.v.w. over 3,500kg but not over 7,500kg [18]

C Vehicles with passenger accommodation for 8 persons or less with a design g.v.w over 3,500kg [18]

D1 Vehicles with passenger accommodation for more than 8 persons but not more than 16 persons [21]

D Vehicles with passenger accommodation for more than 8 persons [21]

Categories EB, EC1, EC, ED1, ED are categories B, C1, C, D1 and D with a trailer attached. The minimum age is the same as for the drawing vehicle. [See notes below]

W Work vehicles and land tractors, with or without a trailer attached [16]

"Passenger accommodation" means seating for passengers in addition to the driver and "design gross vehicle weight" [g.v.w.] means total vehicle weight when laden. This is usually displayed on a metal plate attached to the vehicle.

When going for your test you may be asked to give evidence of the g.v.w. if this is not displayed. Motorcyclists may be asked to show evidence of the engine cylinder capacity of their machine.

NOTES:-

Under the new system a special category EB licence will soon be introduced where a person with a new B category licence intends to draw a heavy trailer. A person who holds a new B licence may draw a light trailer without having to qualify in the EB category.

Details of how the EB category Driving Test will be administered have not yet been finalised and it will be necessary to have a B category licence before you can take that test anyway.

You must hold a Driving Licence for Category B or C1 before you can apply for a Provisional licence for Category C, D or D1.

A person who holds an "old" class C Driving licence may apply for a Driving licence for categories B, C1, EB, EC1 and W.

Provisional licences are now valid for 2 years instead of one and they cost £12. Driving licences will be valid for 10 years [cost £20] or 3 years [cost £12]. A 1 year licence is available in certain cases.

PROVISIONAL LICENCES

If you have NO previous driving experience you may only apply for a Provisional Licence for Category A1, B, C1 or W. Your completed application form for a Provisional Licence must include two Passport photographs, signed on the back. A birth certificate must be included, unless you hold a current Provisional or Driving licence or have held one of these within the last five years or else you hold a valid licence from another member state of the E.C. or from a recognised country.

If you have a current Provisional licence or Driving Licence, then this must be included. If you are renewing an "old" Provisional licence you may apply for the "new" category appropriate to the "old" class of vehicle you drive. The restrictions for new Provisional licence holders do not apply in this case. If in doubt your nearest Licensing Authority will clarify the situation for you.

Certain disabilities automatically disqualify a person from holding a licence. However, a person who suffers from alcoholism, diplopia (double vision), defective binocular vision, epilepsy or severe renal deficiency may, on production of a satisfactory medical report, be granted a licence. Details of requirements for medical certificates are on licence application forms.

It is no longer necessary to apply separately in advance for a Certificate of Fitness as used to be the case.

All applicants for Category A1, A, B, EB or W Provisional licences must undergo a once-off eye test [Form D509]. At present it is also necessary to undergo an eye test when applying for the Driving Test, but this will be phased out. So, to save yourself any inconvenience why not have both forms [D509 and D401] completed by your optician or G.P. at the same time? Remember that you are required to sign the forms in his/her presence!

APPLYING FOR THE TEST

The form for a Certificate of Competency [Driving Test] is Form D401 which is green. As well as your name, address and date of birth you are requested to give a contact telephone number. This is very important, as special arrangements may have to be made for your test.

Although there are forty-seven Driving Test Centres around the country, many cannot provide tests for heavy goods and public service vehicles. You will be informed of the Test Centre nearest you where your test can be carried out.

If you live very far from the regular Test Centres and wish to undergo a motorcycle or work-vehicle test, then the Driver Testing Section will arrange your test at a town convenient to you.

The present fee for the Driving Test in categories A1, A, B, EB or W is £25. For categories C1, C, D1 or D it is £40 and for E category vehicles (other than EB) it is £50. These fees reflect the cost of administering the test.

Your completed form and the appropriate fee should be sent to:-

DRIVER TESTING SECTION
GOVERNMENT BUILDINGS
BALLINA
CO. MAYO
TEL:- 096 70677

*It should be noted that there are penalties for giving false or misleading information.

THE DAY OF THE TEST

You are bound to be nervous on the day of your test. This is natural, but as long as you have practised enough, and you know the Rules of the Road and how to apply them, there is no need to be concerned.

You might find it useful to arrange a Pre-Test lesson before you arrive at the Test Centre. This will help to calm your nerves and will reassure you that you are ready to pass the test.

Your tester knows that you are nervous and will make allowances. No matter how you feel do not take drugs or alcohol to calm yourself! Apart from the fact that it is illegal to drive while under the influence of drugs or drink, you will be a danger to yourself, your tester and to other road-users.

You should arrive at the Test Centre about ten minutes before the appointed time. If you arrive late you may forfeit the test, as each tester has a schedule to keep to.

Park legally and safely close to the Test Centre. Go straight to the waiting room, if there is one. Otherwise you should go into the Test Centre and wait until you are called.

Bring the appropriate provisional licence or full licence, depending on the category of vehicle in which you are being tested, with you. You must also be insured to drive the vehicle. Make certain beforehand that you really are insured to drive the vehicle. Your tester will ask you to sign a statement that your vehicle is in roadworthy condition and that you are insured to drive it.

The tester may examine the vehicle to ensure that the indicators, stop-lights, etc. are working. If you are taking the test in a School of Motoring car all the relevant checks will have been carried out beforehand e.g. Oil, Petrol, Tyre-pressures etc. If the car belongs to you or a relative then you should have all these checks done yourself!

Trade plates are not accepted for test purposes.

Tractors and motorcycles are not required to have "L" plates or insurance discs, but they must have a current tax disc.

The Driver Tester is a Department of the Environment official. The tester's job is to find out if you know the Rules of the Road, if you understand your vehicle controls and can use them, if you can drive confidently, competently and safely with proper regard for other road users.

When your test time arrives you will be called from the waiting room by the tester, into another room. You will be directed to a seat. You will be asked to sign the statement relating to vehicle and insurance.

The first part of your test will consist of some oral questions on the Rules of the Road. You will also be asked to identify some road signs.

Your answers should be detailed and accurate. If you are nervous you may find that your mind goes blank. To help you overcome this there is a Quiz in this book. Remember, though, that this is no substitute for studying the Rules of the Road.

You can be sure that you will not be asked any "trick" questions!

Your test will last 45 minutes if you are being tested in a car, on a motorcycle or on a tractor.

(Tests for larger vehicles last longer).

The tester will ask you to lead the way to your vehicle. When you arrive at your vehicle, be courteous and open the passenger door first.

When you sit into your vehicle you should check that your door is locked and that your seat is properly adjusted. Apply your safety belt. Check that your rear view mirror is properly adjusted. You should also check that your handbrake is ON and that the gears are in neutral. This six point check is dealt with in more detail later.

Your tester is not required to wear a safety belt during the test.

You will be instructed to follow a particular route away from the Test Centre.

All instructions should be quite clear, but if you are unsure of what is required, you should ask! You may also ask for an instruction to be repeated. If you are told to turn left and you turn right, you will not necessarily fail the test.

If, however, you suddenly realise that you have made a mistake, you may become flustered and lose your concentration. This lack of concentration could cause you to make errors which would incur test faults. So take heed of what is said to you!

You will be told to drive on the straight for a short while in order to allow you to settle down. Then you will be directed through a series of right and left hand turns and manoeuvres such as turnabout, reverse and hill start.

You are not allowed to chat with your tester. This is in your own interest.

When your test is complete you will be directed back into the Test Centre. The tester will bring you back into the room from which you first started. You will then be told whether or not you have passed.

If you have passed, you will be given a Certificate of Competency. This is valid for 24 months, for all categories of vehicle. If it is lost or destroyed, then it may be replaced. The duplicate Certificate will be the same as the previous one. You must satisfy the issuing authority that you have adequate reason for acquiring a duplicate. You would be well advised to apply for your Full Driving Licence as soon as possible, because if you allow your Certificate of Competency to expire it will NOT be replaced. If this happens you will have to take another test!

Your Certificate of Competency will note whether or not you need to wear corrective lenses, while driving, if your eye test indicates that you should. This information will be recorded on your Driving Licence.

Other information may be similarly recorded e.g. "limited to vehicles adapted for disability of Licensee" or "limited to vehicles with automatic transmission".

If you fail, you will be given a written statement. You will also be given a REPORT OF DRIVING TEST sheet (Form D 103 A) outlining your driving faults as observed by your tester. This will prove useful to you and your instructor. It can be used as a guide for taking the test again. You should re-apply immediately and be determined to pass the next time.

REMEMBER: THE AIM OF THE DRIVING TEST IS TO ESTABLISH THAT YOU KNOW AND UNDERSTAND THE RULES OF THE ROAD, THAT YOU CAN CONTROL YOUR VEHICLE COMPETENTLY AND SAFELY WITH DUE REGARD FOR THE SAFETY AND CONVENIENCE OF OTHER ROAD USERS

REPORT OF DRIVING TEST (Form D 103 A)

This form lists all of the points of driving procedure which may be observed during your test. Your driving will not be observed exactly in the sequence on Form D 103 A, but it is important for you to know what the Driver Tester is looking for.

Faults on the driving test are marked thus:

X   means you have committed a serious fault. (A serious fault is anything which shows that you cannot control your vehicle with due regard for your own safety or the safety of other road users.)

☐   means you have committed more than one serious fault or that the same serious fault has been repeated.

O   means a disqualifying fault. (A disqualifying fault means that you have done something which is either dangerous or potentially dangerous.)

If you incur a disqualifying fault or a series of serious faults you will fail the test.

REASONS FOR TEST FAILURE

According to the Driver Testing Section of the Department of the Environment there are several common faults which lead to failure. These include:

- lack of proper observation.
- lack of control while steering, changing gears, etc.
- incorrect road position when approaching a turn or a bend.
- incorrect position on a turn or a bend.
- incorrect position leaving a turn or a bend.
- incorrect position on a right-hand turn.
- failure to use the rear-view mirror.
- failure to signal, or signalling too late.
- failure to obey road signs and/or road markings.
- failure to yield right of way.
- failure to stop at a Stop sign.

Most test failures seem to result from a series of separate faults or a pattern of similar faults, rather than a single fault like failure to stop at a Stop sign.

You cannot fail because of anything you have done before the test. Your test is based on the tester's observation of your driving during the course of your test.

APPEALS

The Driver Tester is not allowed to discuss the details of your test with you. If you feel hard done by and that you have a genuine case, you may appeal to the District Court. The court may refuse your appeal. If the court is satisfied that your test was not carried out properly, you will be given another test. You will not have to pay another fee.

WHEN YOU HAVE PASSED

After a proper course of instruction, after digesting the Rules of the Road, after reading this book, and after plenty of practice you should pass the test first time round.

When you have passed and have your Certificate of Competency, you may remove your "L" plates.

Be careful, though, as in your excitement your driving may be a little erratic. It would *not* do to crash on the way home!

CANCELLATION

If for some reason, after you have received notification of your test, you find that you are unable to keep your appointment, then you should contact THE DRIVER TESTING SECTION, in Co. Mayo. Telephone 096 70677.

If you do not do so *at least* 10 days prior to your appointment, your test fee will be forfeit, you will have to re-apply and your name will go to the bottom of the list again.

Previously, it was necessary to state when you would be available to take the test. Now it is necessary to state when you are not available.

WAITING LISTS

Because of the large numbers of candidates for Driving Tests in cars, there is a long waiting list. The time from application to test date can be as long as eleven months. For this reason you should apply for your Test right away.

Considering this delay, you should be well ready for your test when it does come around, *and you should pass it!*

If you genuinely feel that you are not ready, then postpone your test, take some more lessons and get as much practice as you can.

The Department recently increased the number of Driving Testers and reintroduced Saturday testing. These measures should help to reduce the waiting lists.

The waiting list for Heavy Goods and Public Service Vehicles tends to be shorter than for car test. It may be possible to get an appointment within 6 to 10 weeks. This is because of the possibility of employment for those who hold Full Driving Licences for commercial vehicles.

REMEMBER: YOUR 'L' PLATES AND TAX & INSURANCE DISCS.
• LISTEN CAREFULLY AND DO WHAT YOU ARE TOLD.
• YOUR TESTER'S JOB IS TO PASS YOU AND GIVE YOU A CERTIFICATE OF COMPETENCY. YOU WILL ONLY FAIL IF YOU SHOW THAT YOU DO NOT DESERVE TO PASS!
• BECAUSE OF THE E. C. DIRECTIVE IN 1980, THERE WILL NEVER BE ANOTHER AMNESTY FOR PROVISIONAL LICENCE HOLDERS. SO, WHETHER YOU ARE ON YOUR FIRST OR THIRD PROVISIONAL LICENCE, YOU WILL HAVE TO PASS THE TEST BEFORE YOU ARE GRANTED A FULL LICENCE.

ON THE
OPEN ROAD

E very time you sit into a vehicle to drive, you should carry out the following 6 Point Check:

1. DOORS
Improperly closed doors can swing open as you are driving and can be a source of danger to you and others. If you have children or elderly people on board you should check the doors for them. Use child-proof locks if they are fitted to your vehicle.

2. SEAT
Adjust the driver's seat so that you can reach the footpedals with ease. Your seat should not lean too far back as this may restrict your view.

3. SAFETY BELT
Adjust your safety belt so that your movement is not too restricted. Make sure that while you are wearing it you can comfortably steer and change gear. Driver testers are exempt from wearing safety belts while they are conducting tests.

4. MIRRORS

Adjust your mirror(s) so that you can see clearly. If your rear view mirror is properly adjusted you should be able to see clearly out of the rear windscreen. Keep mirrors and windscreens free of dirt and grease. This reduces potential blind spots.

5. HANDBRAKE

The hand brake is a very important piece of equipment in your car. It should always be *on* when your vehicle is parked!

6. THE GEARS

In vehicles with manual gear-shift you should always start up in neutral. This also applies if your engine cuts out in traffic.

MOVING OFF

As you prepare to move away from the kerb, you should always:
- Check in your rear-view mirror.
- Signal your intention.
- Check in your mirror again.
- Look over your right shoulder, this is very important.
- Move away from the kerb, giving way as appropriate.
- Cancel your signal.

ROAD AND LANE POSITIONING

Many motorists ignore road markings. You cannot afford to! Doing so could cost you your test! From the start, you must learn correct positioning. In normal straight driving you should keep your vehicle near the left-hand kerb. Not too close, though, in case you bump the kerb! One way to judge the correct distance is to keep a little to the right of the shore gratings on the road.

THE CORRECT LANE

Here is a guide to finding the correct lane:

If there is only room for single lane traffic then the correct position is the same as outlined above.

If there are two lanes you should keep in the left-hand lane unless you intend turning right or overtaking and have indicated this.

If there are three lanes you should keep in the left-hand lane unless you are turning right or overtaking and have indicated this.

Occasionally you will come across four lanes. In this instance you will usually find filter lanes to the left and right.

If there is a left filter lane and you are going straight ahead then you should be in the lane which is second from the left. The white arrow markings must be obeyed.

When the road markings show three lanes again move back into the left lane as appropriate. If the left lane is blocked by parked vehicles stay in the centre lane.

REMEMBER THE SEQUENCE: DOOR, SEAT, SAFETY BELT, MIRROR, HANDBRAKE AND GEARS. MIRROR, SIGNAL, MIRROR, MANOEUVRE.

KEEP YOUR DISTANCE

Never drive too close to the vehicle in front of you.

This is especially important when road or weather conditions are bad.

Stay well back when you intend to overtake. In this way you will have a clear view of the road ahead.

STOPPING DISTANCES

Your stopping distance depends on:
1. The speed of your reaction - normally almost 1 second.
2. The condition of your brakes.
3. The condition and air pressure of your tyres.
4. The road surface.
5. Weather conditions.
6. The size and weight of your vehicle.
7. The speed at which you are travelling. (3, 4, 5 and 7 can lead to skidding!)

Tail-gaiting is a dangerous habit to acquire and you will usually be held liable if you collide with the rear of another vehicle. Vehicles with anti-lock brakes stop very quickly.

DUAL CARRIAGEWAYS

On a dual carriageway you should keep in the left lane unless you have to overtake or turn right and have signalled your intention. The outer lane on a two-lane carriageway is for faster traffic. If there are three lanes you should avoid the outer lane except for overtaking or turning right.

Some motorists treat dual carriageways as if they were motorways. This is extremely dangerous as restricted access and restricted speed limits apply on dual carriageways unlike on motorways.

JUNCTIONS
AND INTERSECTIONS

ROADS OF EQUAL IMPORTANCE

When approaching roads of equal importance, check in your rear-view mirror, slow down slightly and keep a good lookout for potential hazards. Look carefully into the junction and only proceed if it is safe to do so. Look right and left as you go.

WHEN APPROACHING ROADS OF EQUAL IMPORTANCE YOU MUST GIVE WAY TO TRAFFIC COMING FROM YOUR RIGHT.

MAJOR TO MINOR ROADS

Although you have the right of way you must be very observant. Expect the unexpected at this type of junction as the entrance may be partially concealed. Slow down as appropriate.

MINOR TO MAJOR ROADS

Whenever you approach this type of junction you can expect to find a Yield Right of Way sign, a Stop sign or traffic lights. There will usually be a solid white line across your side of the junction. If, however, you approach a Stop sign where there is no line, you must stop close to the sign itself. "Dribbling through" at the junction is not permitted. You must stop.

When turning left at a junction you should position your vehicle so that you have the best possible view of the road to your right. Do this by keeping left as you move up to the line.

When entering a major road from a minor road you must exercise extreme caution! This also applies when you are coming out of a private residence, car park or other area off the main road.

ONE-WAY STREET SYSTEMS

In a one-way street system you should position your vehicle correctly. The correct position will depend on the direction you intend to take at the end of the street.

If, for example, you have been told to turn to the right you should position your vehicle in the right-hand lane.Watch out for changes in the traffic flow .i.e. two-way traffic, when the one-way system ends.

ROUNDABOUTS

You will see this sign as you approach a roundabout.

Recently a new roadmarking has been introduced. It is a white triangle painted on the road as you approach the roundabout.

It has the same meaning as a Yield Right of Way sign.

REMEMBER:ALWAYS LOOK RIGHT, LEFT AND RIGHT AGAIN AT JUNCTIONS

There are single and double lane round-abouts. If there are two lanes you should choose the lane which suits you, but avoid cutting in on other vehicles as you do so. You must always enter a roundabout by turning to the left and always give way to traffic coming from the right.

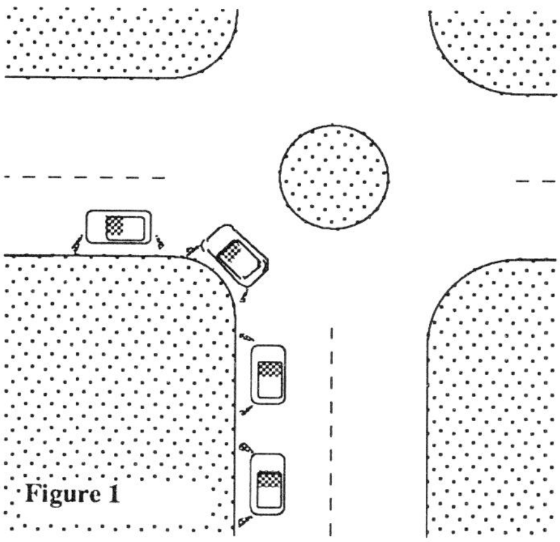

Here is a suggested procedure for negotiating roundabouts:

LEFT TURN: **(See Figure 1.)**
- Keep in the left lane.
- Check in your mirror.
- Indicate left well in advance of the turn.
- Give way to traffic on the roundabout.
- Check in your mirror again.
- Keep in the left lane and exit roundabout.

Figure 1

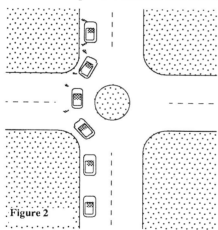

Figure 2

STRAIGHT AHEAD:
(See figure 2.)
- Keep in the left lane.
- Check in your mirror.
- Give way to traffic on the roundabout.
- Check in your mirror.
- Only indicate left when you have passed the centre of the first exit.
- Check in your mirror again.
- Keep in the left lane and exit roundabout.

Note: You may use the right hand lane if traffic conditions dictate, but you must exercise extreme caution.

RIGHT TURN: **(see figure 3.)**
- Mirror/Signal/Mirror/Manoeuvre into the right-hand lane approaching the roundabout.
- Give way to traffic on the roundabout.
- Check in your mirror.
- Leave right indicator on.

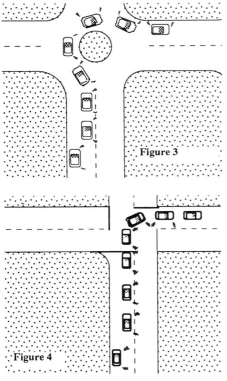

.·Figure 3

·Figure 4

- As you reach the centre of the second exit use your mirror and signal left.
- Check in your mirror again, proceed with caution.
- Move into the left lane and exit roundabout.

TURNING RIGHT AT A JUNCTION

This manoeuvre often causes problems for learner drivers. (**See Figure 4**) As you approach a junction where you intend to turn right you should:

- Mirror/ Signal/ Mirror/ Manoeuvre into the right-hand lane, just left of the centre of the road. Do this in good time, well in advance of the junction.
- Leave your right indicator on.
- Slow down as you approach the junction.
- Give way to traffic coming from the opposite direction which is going straight through or which is turning left. Stop if necessary.
- Check in your mirror before turning right.
- Always move around the centre of the junction.
- You must not overshoot or cut the corner.
- Check in your mirror again.
- Go directly into the left lane.

Unless the road markings or traffic signals show otherwise, ideally, you should not turn right in front of another vehicle. The correct procedure is for both vehicles to pass behind each other. This means offside to offside but this rarely happens.

When you are on test try to carry out this manoeuvre correctly. Some motorists will not co-operate with you. It is acceptable for you to pass in front of the other vehicle if you have no other option. Remember to observe very carefully and take great care. Use your own best judgement in this. Your tester will take account of the traffic conditions.

Whatever you do don't block the junction! If there is a yellow box on the junction do not enter unless your exit road is clear.

REMEMBER: IF THE LEFT HAND LANE IS BLOCKED AS YOU APPROACH EITHER A ROUNDABOUT OR ANOTHER JUNCTION YOU SHOULD MOVE INTO THE RIGHT-HAND LANE. PROCEED WITH EXTREME CAUTION!

TURNING LEFT AT A JUNCTION

- Approach the junction in the left lane.
- Check in your mirror.
- Signal your intention to turn in good time, well in advance of the junction.

If, you are told to take the second next turn to the left, then you must not signal until you have passed the centre of the first turn. (See **Figure** **5**)

- Slow down and change down from 4th gear.
- You should usually corner in 2nd gear, giving way to pedestrians if necessary. Change gear *before* you reach the corner.
- Check in your mirror,
- Keep as close to the kerb as practicable, when turning.
- Do not mount or bump the kerb.
- Do not swing wide.
- Check in your mirror again.
- Move directly into the left lane.
- Maintain reasonable progress.

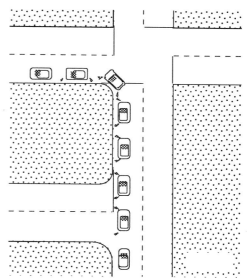

STOPPING

When you stop your vehicle it should be in a safe position. You should avoid stopping where you will cause an obstruction. Take great care when stopping at the kerb.

- Check in your mirror.
- Indicate your intention.
- Slow down, changing gear as necessary.
- Check in your mirror again.
- Stop close to the kerb.
- Apply the handbrake.
- Put the gears in neutral.

Use the foot pedals in this order:
1. Right foot off the accelerator.
2 Right foot presses the brake.
3. Left foot on the clutch only when vehicle is almost stopped and just before the engine stalls and cuts out.

EMERGENCY STOPS

An emergency stop is not part of the driving test in this country. If you find that in the course of your test you have to make an emergency stop, then hold the steering wheel steady. Brake firmly, keeping a steady pressure to help prevent the brakes from locking. Pumping the brakes can also help. Only use the clutch as the vehicle stops. When you have stopped, apply the handbrake. Put the gears into neutral. Observe all around you before you move off again. Don't forget to use your mirror, to signal and to look over your right shoulder as you move off.

OTHER ROAD USERS

It is an enormous responsibility to be in charge of a vehicle.

You have a right to drive, but there are duties that attend that right.

When you are motoring, you must take account of the danger you present to other road users.

PEDESTRIANS

Pedestrians of all ages are unpredictable, but children are especially so. Drivers must give way to pedestrians at all times. Motorists must never place pedestrians at risk no matter how antagonistic they may be. The intention of pedestrians who jay-walk may be to make you angry. Pedestrians should not behave in this way but unfortunately some do, often without realising the danger!

Be especially careful if your test is being carried out near a school or playground.

It is worth noting the behaviour of pedestrians as they cross the road in busy traffic. They make a dash towards the centre of the roadway. Then they make for the other pavement, but you should observe how they slow down! Pedestrians in charge of a buggy or a pram have a tendency to turn off the pavement suddenly. They seem to forget how dangerous this is and may push the buggy into the path of oncoming traffic.

Always expect this to happen and be prepared to slow down or stop.

Drivers must give way to pedestrians at zebra crossings, pelican crossings, and pedestrian lights. If a pedestrian is already crossing the road or is crossing at a junction as you approach they have right of way. This applies whether you are starting off from the kerb or motoring along.

CYCLISTS AND MOTORCYCLISTS

Cyclists and motorcyclists are often invisible to motorists. This is because of their small size and because of the number of blind spots in any vehicle. Cyclists and motorcyclists, even though they should, rarely look around before manoeuvring. They often overtake parked vehicles without taking account of the danger they pose. When the weather is bad these road users are especially vulnerable. They can easily be blown into the path of following vehicles. It is also important for motorists not to cut in on this group of road users. Motorists should be especially careful as they open the door of their vehicle, when parked.

REMEMBER: BRAKE FIRST --- THEN CLUTCH!

ANIMAL TRAFFIC

Persons in charge of animals have the right to signal you to slow down or stop. Even if you are not given such a signal, you must slow down anyway and be prepared to stop. Take extra care when overtaking animals.

OVERTAKING / PASSING

When approaching stationary vehicles you should glance under their wheels. In this way you may see a pedestrian's feet, even if he or she is not tall enough to be seen above the vehicle itself. If a ball, or a similar object, is thrown into the roadway you should not watch it. You should watch out for the child who may be following it. Remember that although most children know the Safe Cross Code, they may forget to apply it, in the excitement of play,

When you are overtaking, you should not be too close to the vehicle in front of you. Move out smoothly and give plenty of clearance. If you have to change lanes or cross the centre line of the road, you must signal your intention. When you are moving back into the correct lane, you must not cut in. The best way of making sure that you have given sufficient clearance is to use your rear-view mirror. When you can see what you have overtaken, in your mirror, then you can move in again.

You may not overtake if it is dangerous to do so. You must wait. For example, you must not overtake at a corner, on a bend, at the brow of a hill, on a hump-backed bridge, where there are zig-zag markings at pedestrian lights, at pelican or zebra crossings, at traffic lights or other junctions or where you might cause danger or inconvenience to other road users.

Remember also that you must not cross a continuous white line to overtake. You may only cross a broken white line if it is safe to do so and you have signalled your intention. HATCHED markings have recently been introduced. These are diagonal white stripes. They separate oncoming traffic or form a traffic island if you are turning right. Following traffic may not overtake you if this means driving over the marked area. (See **Figure 6**).

OVERTAKING ON THE LEFT

Overtaking is normally carried out on the right, but you may overtake on the left:

(a)   When the motorist in front intends turning right and you are going straight on or left.

(b)   When you are turning left and have indicated this.

(c)   In slow moving traffic, when you are in the left lane and the traffic in the lane to your right is not moving as fast as the traffic in your lane.

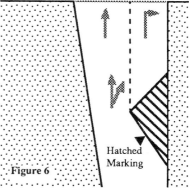

Figure 6

Hatched Marking

You may find in city driving, that the left lane is almost totally free of traffic. This is because many motorists fail to read the road ahead and simply follow the vehicle in front of them. Traffic jams are often caused because of this.

OVERTAKING ON THE RIGHT

When you are overtaking on the right you should allow sufficient room for a clear view. Only manoeuvre if you have the speed and the power to do so. Never accelerate when another vehicle is overtaking you.

ANTICIPATION / OBSERVATION

Look around you when moving off, changing lanes, overtaking, turning about, or reversing. Look right and left approaching junctions, at roundabouts, and as you enter another road. When pulling into the kerb or turning left make sure it is safe to do so. Be especially observant of pedestrians and cyclists between you and the kerb when pulling in or turning left. It can be fatal to follow blindly behind another vehicle, especially if it is overtaking.

READING THE ROAD AHEAD

Read the road ahead and anticipate what other road users may do. Many motorists manoeuvre or change lanes without any signals whatsoever. You often have to be a mind reader so be observant and *expect the unexpected.*

If a hazard does arise you should react correctly. Either slow down or stop. Sound your horn if necessary.

Reading the road consists of being aware of what is going on all around your vehicle. This means looking immediately in front, into the middle distance and well ahead of you. You must also look in your mirror.

MIRROR

Use of your rear-view and side mirrors are essential to good, safe motoring. Ideally you should check your rear-view mirror every 20 or 25 seconds. Use your mirror before and after you signal that you intend to move off, change lanes, turn left or right, carry out any manoeuvre, slow down or stop.

You may not be aware of it, but the Driver Tester is ideally positioned to monitor your use or non use of the rear view mirror.

BLIND SPOTS

Look at the diagram and you will see how many blind spots there are in a motor car. There are bigger blind spots on bigger vehicles. Don't add to them by having dirty mirrors or windscreens. Stickers or badges, including "L" plates increase the number of blind spots. Ideally your "L" plates should be placed on the body of your vehicle. Cushions, toys, stickers and "dangly things" may look nice when attached to mirrors and windscreens, but they are potentially dangerous. They may distract you or obstruct your view.

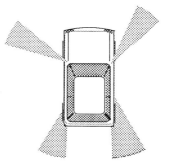

SIGNALS

Your indicators should be used correctly and you should always signal your intention in good time. You must signal when you are moving off, changing lanes, overtaking, at roundabouts, turning right or left, slowing, or pulling in at the side of the road.

Don't forget to cancel your signal. Even though most indicators cancel automatically they will only do so if the steering wheel turns beyond a certain point. Under the pressure of the test you may forget to cancel an indication made, and incur a test fault.

THE HORN

Your horn is a warning signal. Except in an emergency you should not sound your horn between 11. 30 at night and 7 o'clock in the morning. Overuse or aggressive use of the horn may lead to a test fault, but if you do not use it when you should, you can also incur test faults.

Take into account that a pedestrian or cyclist who is deaf, or indeed using a Walkman, may not hear your horn.

Helpful use of the horn will indicate to other road users that there is danger about.

HAND SIGNALS

You will usually be asked to demonstrate hand signals at some convenient spot during the test. The tester will ask you to show the appropriate signals to be given to other motorists and to a pointsman on duty.

SIGNALS TO OTHER TRAFFIC	SIGNALS TO A POINTSMAN
I intend to move off / turn right.	I intend to turn right.
I intend to turn left. (move arm anti clockwise).	I intend to turn left.
I intend to slow down / stop.	I intend to go straight on.

REMEMBER NEITHER FLASHING YOUR INDICATOR NOR SOUNDING YOUR HORN GIVES YOU THE RIGHT OF WAY.

RIGHT OF WAY

When you are moving off, changing lanes, overtaking, at a junction or roundabout, turning left or right, slowing down or stopping, you must give way to other road users.

Be especially aware of pedestrians, cyclists, motorcyclists, horse-drawn vehicles and persons in charge of animals and yield right of way as appropriate.

You must stop at a Stop sign. Stop at the line or sign. Give way to traffic coming from either direction. At a Yield Right of Way sign slow down and stop if necessary. Yield right of way to traffic coming from either direction. Even if there is no sign and you are entering a major road - Give Way.

When turning right (see road and lane position) give way to traffic coming from the opposite direction. The oncoming vehicle has right of way if you are turning right, and it is going straight on or turning left.

- Give way to pedestrians as appropriate.
- Give way to traffic on the main road if you are coming out of a driveway, car park, garage or other private entrance.
- Give way in order to avoid inconvenience to other road users.
- Give way to Gardai, Ambulance, and Fire Brigade vehicles if they display blue flashing lights or sound their sirens.

PROGRESS

It takes a lot of practice to judge the appropriate speed for moving off, driving on the straight, at junctions and at yield signs. Remember not to stop unless you have to. The same applies as you are entering roundabouts and turning either right or left. You must not cause an obstruction, especially at junctions. Busy junctions with traffic lights are notoriously difficult for learner drivers.

SPEED

Speed limit signs show the maximum speed at which you may travel. You should keep up to the speed limit only if it is safe to do so. In city driving the maximum speed is 30 m.p.h. in built-up areas and 40 to 50 m.p h. on some busy main roads. Outside the speed limit area the maximum speed allowed is 55 m.p.h.

Maximum speed limits also apply to certain vehicles (see Rules of the Road booklet for details.)

Adjust your speed to suit your manoeuvre especially when approaching junctions, roundabouts, traffic lights, pedestrian and pelican crossings. Always be prepared to slow down, stop or give way as necessary. You must take account of road, traffic and weather conditions.

TRAFFIC CONTROLS

Traffic lights may be the bane of road users lives, but they must be obeyed!
Red means stop behind the line.
Amber means stop unless it is unsafe to do so.
Green means go, only if the junction is clear
and it is safe for you to proceed.
A flashing amber light at a pelican crossing,
means you may only proceed if there is no
pedestrian on the crossing.

Green arrows, like white arrow markings on the roadway, indicate that you must go in that direction. That is why it is so important to read the road ahead and get into the correct lane before you reach the junction.

Move into the correct lane and position at junctions when (a) turning left (b) going straight on or (c) turning right.

You must obey the signals of Gardai, School Wardens and persons in charge of animals. You must also obey the signals of flag-men at roadworks or other obstructions.

If you intend going straight ahead where there is a filter-light to the left, you must move into the right-hand lane.

BROKEN TRAFFIC LIGHTS

If the lights are broken proceed as if they are red.
Stop behind the line and observe carefully.
The decision to proceed is yours alone.
When you are satisfied that it is safe to do so you should proceed with caution.

VEHICLE CONTROLS

You must maintain full control of your vehicle at all times. This is achieved by proper use of the accelerator, the footbrake, the clutch, the gears, the handbrake and the steering.

THE ACCELERATOR

You must use the accelerator smoothly and avoid "roaring" the engine between gear changes or while stopped in traffic

THE CLUTCH

It is forbidden to use the clutch other than for changing gears and for disengaging the gears just before you stop.
In order to prove to yourself how dangerous coasting can be, try this exercise - :
Find a quiet stretch of road and using lamp-posts as a guide, start off in first gear.

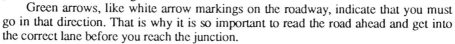

REMEMBER:YOU CAN FAIL THE TEST EITHER FOR DRIVING OVER CAUTIOUSLY OR FOR TRAVELLING FASTER THAN IS SAFE IN THE CIRCUMSTANCES. YOU WILL INCUR TEST FAULTS FOR EXCEEDING THE SPEED LIMIT.

Then hold the clutch down and see just how far your vehicle will go before it coasts to a halt. This exercise is to impress upon you that you must always use the brake before using the clutch

Coasting with the clutch down and/or rolling along in neutral are dangerous driving habits to acquire.

While driving, the best position for your left foot is flat on the floor, slightly to the left of the clutch pedal. Only raise your foot to the clutch pedal when you intend to change gear or stop. Resting your foot on the clutch-pedal or "riding" the clutch can cause unnecessary wear on the clutch itself.

A simple rule to remember is: *don't press the clutch and acelerator together i.e. off the accelerator - on the clutch - off the clutch - on the accelerator.*

If you keep the clutch and accelerator pedals down at the same time, you will cause the engine to roar. This simply wastes petrol! There is a fine balance between the point where the clutch engages and disengages. With practice you will find this.

THE GEARS

Smooth gear changing takes practice. On your first few lessons your instructor may only allow you to use the first three gears. As you gain confidence you will be encouraged to use fourth gear.

A good habit to acquire is that of moving your left hand and left foot at the same time during gear changes.

Once you've changed gear take your foot off the clutch and return your left hand to the correct position on the steering wheel.

CHOOSING THE CORRECT GEAR.

Neutral: Your vehicle should always be in neutral when you start up the engine, when restarting if your vehicle cuts out in traffic, if you expect a long delay in traffic and when you have parked.

You may leave the vehicle in gear, while the engine is off, when you are parked on a steep incline.

First Gear : This is for starting off, or for when you are stopped in traffic ready to move off. (Speed 0 - 10 m.p.h. approx.)

Second Gear: This gear is used as you build up speed. It is also used when you are cornering. There is no need to go down to second gear when stopping. (Speed 5 - 15m. p. h. up to a maximum of 28 - 30 m.p.h. approx.)

Third Gear: This is for building up speed or slowing down. It may be used as you reduce speed approaching traffic lights, pedestrian crossings, roundabouts or junctions or when approaching an obvious hazard. You are more in control in this gear than in fourth gear. (Speed 15 - 25 m. p. h. up to a maximum of 48 - 50 m.p.h. approx.)

2nd and 3rd gears may be used to give greater control when you are driving down a steep hill.

COASTING ALONG WITH THE CLUTCH DOWN OR PUTTING THE CLUTCH DOWN WHEN CORNERING IS DANGEROUS. IT MEANS YOU ARE NOT IN CONTROL OF YOUR VEHICLE.

You should usually stop in third gear having changed down from fourth. If you are already in third gear, you may stop in third gear, but you may prefer to change down to second. This is acceptable procedure. Do *not* change down to first to stop!

Fourth Gear: This is the top gear on most vehicles and is used for driving at speed. You may stop in fourth gear when you are unable to change down through the gears in time. This might occur as you reach traffic-lights which change to red quickly. It would also apply in an emergency. You have less control over your vehicle in high gear.

Fifth Gear: (Speeds over 25 m. p. h.) Some vehicles have a fifth or " overdrive " gear which allows for "cruising" at speed on the open road. It is not generally used in slow, city traffic conditions. You are unlikely to need 5th gear when taking the test, although there is no reason not to use it if the situation warrants it and you feel confident about doing so.

An important aspect of gear changing is not to labour the engine. Practise choosing the correct gear for the situation. For example: Don't try to drive up a steep hill in high gear. It causes undue strain on the engine and it could cause you to stall.

Practise starting off in first gear until you are confident that you will not stall or cut out. Continuous cutting out will go against you on your test.

THE BRAKES

Your footbrake must always be applied smoothly, except in emergencies. You must not use the footbrake too much when cornering. You may "cover" the brake when cornering and only apply pressure as necessary.

THE HANDBRAKE

You should use the handbrake when parked or when stopped in traffic and during the Turnabout. Your vehicle must *not* roll forward or backward. Apply and release the handbrake smoothly.

STEERING

You must hold the steering wheel where it gives you maximum control. This is between a quarter to three and ten minutes to two on the clock. When reversing, the position changes to five past seven on the clock.

You must have both hands on the steering wheel at all times except when changing gear and signalling. You must keep the steering wheel steady and avoid wobbles in the steering. This may take some practice but will come in time.

Crossing Hands: You must never cross hands one over the other. This signifies a lack of control.

When turning the steering wheel always push up with the right hand and pull down with the left. Push up with the left and pull down with the right.

NEVER ALLOW THE STEERING WHEEL TO SLIP THROUGH YOUR FINGERS.

REVERSING

The ability to reverse your vehicle safely is a very important skill. It is particularly useful for parking in a narrow space. However, it takes a considerable amount of practice. On your driving test you will be expected to reverse to the left while keeping reasonably close to the kerb. You must not bump or mount the kerb. Nor must you swing too wide. As you reverse, try not to travel too slowly. Manoeuvre smartly. You must take proper observation and give way to traffic coming up behind your vehicle. Stop if necessary. Observation is the key note of this manoeuvre. You must be aware of everything that is going on around you. You must also maintain complete control over your vehicle using the accelerator, the clutch, the footbrake, the handbrake and the steering wheel.

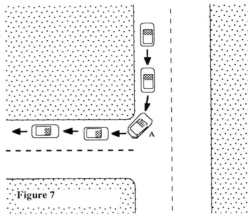

Figure 7

Here are some suggested approaches to the reversing manoeuvre. On your test you will be told to "Pull in at the kerb, just beyond the next left turn. "

- Use your mirror and watch out for cyclists or motorcyclists coming up on your left.
- Signal your intention to pull in when you have passed the centre of the left turn.
- Check in the mirror again.
- Park parallel to the kerb.
- You will have been told by your tester or you will have realised that the reversing manoeuvre is next.
- Allow for this and park a little further out from the kerb than usual. Not too far out, though, as you could incur a penalty.
- Stop the vehicle, apply the handbrake and go into neutral.
- Do not switch off the engine unless told otherwise.

- If in doubt ask!

When told to reverse:
- Release your safety belt. This is allowed.
- Start your engine if you had switched it off earlier.
- Select reverse gear smoothly, without crunching. You can avoid crunching the gears by keeping your right foot OFF the accelerator.
- Release your handbrake and begin reversing while looking over your left shoulder. Looking in the rear view mirror will not do!

REMEMBER: WHEN REVERSING - YOU DO NOT HAVE RIGHT OF WAY!

- Keep both hands on the steering wheel - right hand high up, left hand low down..
- Ease the clutch up and down to control the speed of your manoeuvre. Use the accelerator as little as possible.
- When your rear wheels approach the corner, gently turn the steering wheel to the left.
- As you round the corner the rear passenger wheel will go towards the kerb a little. Don't straighten up too soon or you will end up too far out from the kerb. Remember though, you must not swing too wide or bump or mount the kerb. Straighten up by gently feeding the steering wheel right.
- When you reach the apex of the corner and the front wheels of your vehicle move outwards, the offside wing will be exposed. It is most important that you look to your right at this point, and all about you. (See A in Figure 7).
- When you have straightened your vehicle parallel to the kerb, you must continue to reverse until you are told to stop. This is to assess your control over the vehicle as you reverse.
- Check all the time for hazards or potential hazards. Give way as necessary.
- Stop only when told to, apply the handbrake and choose neutral.
- When told to drive on re-apply your safety belt before moving away from the kerb in the usual way.

WARNING: If you are near the corner and are told to turn left you must first indicate right because you are moving off. Then indicate left for the turn.

This manoeuvre takes a considerable amount of practice. You should find a quiet spot and try it again and again. Do not expect to reverse perfectly right away. It may seem that you will never get it right, but you will IN TIME!

TURNABOUT

This manoeuvre is commonly known as the 3 POINT TURN. On test you do not have to turnabout in only three moves. If you are driving a short vehicle you should be able to turn your vehicle completely about in three moves. Even if you drive a large vehicle you will usually be asked to carry out this manoeuvre in a road where three moves will do.

But 5 or more moves are allowed, so don't panic!

- Remember that your tester is looking for confident and competent handling of the vehicle.
- You are not allowed to bump the kerb or drive onto the pavement.
- You must observe properly and be considerate of other road users.
- You must carry out the manoeuvre at a reasonable speed and you must be in complete control of your vehicle.
- As with reversing, you must practise this manoeuvre.
  Some things to remember about the turnabout:
- Remember the shape of the road surface. Use your handbrake each time you stop to make sure that your tyres don't bump the kerb either as you go forward or reverse.

- Look at your vehicle and see exactly where the wheels are. Notice how much space there is between the bonnet and the front wheels and the boot and the rear wheels.
- If you roll down your window before you start the turnabout, then you can get a better view of your position as you reverse during the manoeuvre.
- If it has been raining use a cloth to wipe your windscreens before manoeuvring. Before setting out wipe inside windscreens with a cloth which has been dampened with shampoo or washing- up liquid. This will help prevent your windows fogging-up during the test.

TURNING IN THREE POINTS OR MORE

Point One:

- Position your vehicle parallel to and close to the kerb.
- Do not bump the kerb.
- Apply the handbrake, go into neutral.
- Roll down your window.
- Select first gear.
- Release the handbrake.
- Check in your mirror, signal and check your mirror again.
- Proceed if it safe to do so!
- Look over your right shoulder.
- Give way to traffic or pedestrians, as appropriate.
- Turn the steering wheel fully to the right only when you have begun to move.
- Before you reach the centre of the roadway you should have the *full lock on*!
- As you approach the opposite kerb put the *left lock on!* This will give you an advantage as you reverse.
- Apply your handbrake to avoid rolling.
- Observe *right, left, in your mirror* and *right* again.
- Make sure it is safe to proceed.

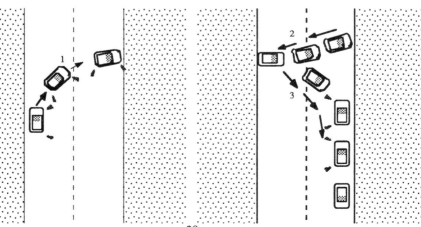

- Give way to traffic coming from your right.
- If a driver to your left is anxious to get going - allow him/her to proceed, if it is safe to do so.

Point Two:

- Choose reverse gear and release the handbrake.
- Don't allow the vehicle to roll and bump the kerb.
- Carefully, and observing all round, reverse towards the kerb from which you started out.
- Avoid bumping the kerb. Do this by looking out the open window to see how close you are to the kerb.
- Apply the handbrake.
- Continue to observe and be courteous to other road users.

Point Three:

- Select first gear and indicate.
- Release the handbrake.
- *Don't roll backwards!*
- Proceed only if it is safe to do so.
- Put on the *full right lock*.
- Proceed towards the opposite kerb.
- Move directly into the left lane and continue unless told to do otherwise.
- Check in your mirror.
- Acknowledge the courtesy of other motorists with a smile and a nod rather than by removing a hand from the steering wheel to wave.

PARKING

You must park correctly and safely. You must only park where it is legal to do so. You may not park too close to a corner, on a corner, a bend, near the brow of a hill, the summit of a hump-backed bridge, opposite a continuous white line where there are fewer than three lanes, near a pedestrian or pelican crossing, at traffic lights, in a clearway or on a single yellow line during restricted times, on a double yellow line, in a taxi rank or a space reserved for loading or for buses. You must not double or triple park, or place your vehicle where it will cause any inconvenience or obstruction to other road users.

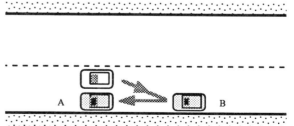

REMEMBER: IF YOU DON'T MANAGE THE TURNABOUT IN THREE MOVES REPEAT POINTS 2 AND 3 AS NECESSARY.

When you are parking, you may not find it possible to drive directly into a parking spot. It is very often necessary to reverse into position, usually between two vehicles.

This is another manoeuvre which takes practice. Remember that you do not have right of way when reversing. Be especially considerate of cyclists and pedestrians. This manoeuvre is not part of the test.

Here is a suggested technique for reversing into a position .
- Follow the proper procedure and stop parallel to the vehicle marked A.
- Reverse until the front windscreen of your vehicle draws level with the rear windscreen of Vehicle A.
- Lock gently to the left.
- As the left rear wheel approaches the kerb, lock the steering to the right.
- Stop before your rear bumper touches the front bumper of vehicle B.
- Straighten into parking position. Apply handbrake, choose neutral. Switch off engine.

Check in your mirror and look over your right shoulder when you intend opening your door.

COURTESY

A discourteous driver is a potentially dangerous driver. Courtesy on the road costs nothing, but it pays great dividends. A courteous driver will, for example, never block a junction cutting off another driver's access or exit route. Your driving should be defensive rather than aggressive. In other words - *Watch out for the Wallies!*

In order to drive well and safely you do *not* have to be antagonistic towards other road users.

On test you will be required to show proper regard for the safety and convenience of other road users.

This does not mean that when you pass the test you can forget the Rules of the Road.

THE HILL START

At some point during your test, you will be asked to demonstrate a hillstart. This is a manoeuvre which will show your ability to correctly move off from the kerb on an incline. This manoeuvre demands clutch control and co-ordination.

Here is a suggested technique for the hillstart.
- When you are directed to park at the kerb on a hill you should mirror signal/mirror/manoeuvre in the usual way.
- As you bring your vehicle to a halt, you should apply the handbrake before going into neutral.
- At this point of the test you may be asked to demonstrate the hand signals (See Hand Signals page 23).
- Roll down your window fully, so you can demonstrate the hand signals correctly.

REMEMBER: YOUR DRIVING SHOULD BE DEFENSIVE RATHER THAN AGGRESSIVE

- When told to proceed you should roll your window up *before* moving off.
- Switch on the engine if you have switched it off earlier.
- Select first gear.
- Check in your mirror, signal, check in your mirror again and look over your right shoulder as you move away from the kerb.
- In order to make sure that your vehicle does not roll back, you should press the accelerator a little more than usual.

Listen to the sound of the engine revs. As you ease up the clutch you will hear the "revs" die down as the clutch is about to engage.
- This is the point at which you should release the handbrake and proceed away from the kerb, if it is safe to do so.
- This same procedure may be used if you must stop and start on any incline.

KNOWING THE TEST ROUTE

When you have applied for your driving test you will have chosen a particular test centre. You will usually be accommodated in this. Sometimes, however, this may not be possible.

Many driving instructors take their pupils around test routes in order to help them become familiar with the test area. Ideally you should be able to take your test from any centre without knowing the area. Many learner drivers find that it helps their confidence if they are familiar with the test area. If you choose to do this, then it is advisable to familiarise yourself with the various types of junctions, pedestrian and traffic lights, crossings and road markings in the vicinity of the test centre. This should help you to read the road and to anticipate the kind of hazard you may meet while on test.

HEAVY GOODS VEHICLES, PUBLIC SERVICE VEHICLES AND MOTORCYCLES

While the main emphasis of this text has been on the Driving Test for car drivers, much of it also applies to drivers of heavy good vehicles and public service vehicles. There are differences, such as the approach to turning left and right, where an articulated vehicle must straddle two lanes, rather than stay in a particular lane. Another difference is that during the heavy goods vehicles test you will be required to reverse to the right as well as to the left.

Certain technical information is also required of drivers of these larger vehicles, including pressures in air-brakes, maximum height, width, length and weight of loads for heavy goods vehicles. It also includes information about the correct procedures for hitching and un-hitching trailers, the maximum speed limits, the maximum number of driving hours permitted in a 24hr. period and information about the tacograph.

This information is best acquired through an experienced School of Motoring or through a specialised Training Scheme, such as those run by FÁS.

REMEMBER: TEST ROUTES MAY BE CHANGED FROM TIME TO TIME.

MOTORCYCLISTS

Motorcyclists are required to observe the Rules of the Road in a similar way to car drivers. On test they are required to

- Look behind before moving off/overtaking/changing lanes/turning right/ turning left/ slowing down / stopping and at roundabouts.
- Give the correct hand signal as well as using the direction indicator. This must be done in good time, well in advance of the manoeuvre.

Keep the motorcycle well under control while signalling. Both hands must be on the handlebars during the turn.

- Drive at a slow (walking) speed for a short distance, to show control.
- Perform a U-turn properly, observing and signalling correctly.
- Steer a pre-determined course correctly.

ON TEST

The motorcycle test consists of an oral test on the Rules of the Road and the preliminary details about Road Tax and insurance.

The candidate will then be advised of the test route.

The tester will ask the candidate to lead the way to where the motorcycle is parked.

The tester will observe as you carry out the instructions you have been given. You will be directed to make several manoeuvres to show that you can handle your machine capably and safely.

PROTECTION

It is essential for motorcyclists to pay close attention to their own safety and the safety of others.

Crash helmets must always be worn - this is the law!

Protective clothing and footwear are far more important than many motorcyclists seem to think.

Statistics show that 80% of motorcyclists or pillion passengers involved in road traffic accidents are likely to be killed or injured. It also makes sense to keep your machine in good condition.

If you can, you should avail of proper instruction in the handling and maintenance of your machine. This will pay dividends as you prepare for the test and after you have passed.

NEW REGULATIONS

Owing to the alarming statistics relating to motorcycle accidents, new restrictions apply. You will not be granted a Provisional licence for a high powered machine over 150cc [Category A] until you have held a Full Driving licence for a lower powered machine [Category A1] for at least two years. You must be at least 18 years of age before you can qualify on a Category A machine.

The "old" limited Class A licence for mopeds and motorcycles not exceeding 50cc is now extended. They fall into Category A1, which covers motorcycles up to 125cc.

REMEMBER: MOTORCYCLISTS AND THEIR PASSENGERS MUST ALWAYS WEAR CRASH HELMETS. MOTORCYCLISTS WITH A PROVISIONAL LICENCE MAY NOT CARRY A PASSENGER

THE NATIONAL SAFETY COUNCIL

The National Safety Council of 4 Northbrook Road, Ranelagh, Dublin, 6., have a range of very useful booklets for learner drivers.

Four in particular are worth mentioning. They are:

1. The Rules of the Road.
2. A Licence to live?
3. This is your Bike.
4. Road Safety for the Farming Community.

These are available on request. You simply have to cover the cost of the postage.

DISABLED DRIVERS

In January 1970 the **Physically Handicapped and Disabled Drivers Association of Ireland** was founded. It was set up by the late Martin Donoghue and his late wife Ann, along with Pat Grogan who is the present President of the Association. The D.D.A.I. came into being in order to give maximum independence to physically disabled people. The Association is run by disabled people for disabled people.

As well as providing vocational training for the disabled it provides an intensive course in driving instruction at its centre in **Ballindine, Co. Mayo**. There, drivers can be assessed and advice is given to those who are disabled and who are new to driving, or to newly disabled people who want to drive.

Consultation includes advice regarding driving licence and Driving Test application; make and model of vehicle to purchase and vehicle adaptation; motor insurance and a range of other concessions available to the disabled motorist.

The D.D.A.I. motoring course is residential and lasts for three weeks with three hours of instruction per day, five days per week. Disabled drivers taking this course are generally funded by their local Health Board.

When it comes to the Driving Test, disabled drivers are generally tested by a Supervisory Driver Tester. The Driving Test is the same for disabled drivers as it is for everyone else and a certificate of competency is only granted to those who deserve it. It is worth noting that the success rate of disabled motorists is very high, especially among those who have taken the intensive course.

For further information contact:
THE DISABLED DRIVERS ASSOCIATION OF IRELAND
HEAD OFFICE: Ballindine, Co. Mayo. Tel: (094) 64054/64266.
DUBLIN OFFICE: Carmichael House, 4 Nth. Brunswick St, Dublin 8.
Tel:(01)721671.
CORK OFFICE: 6 South Tce., Cork. Tel: (021) 313033.

RULES OF THE ROAD

QUIZ

It has already been stated that the first part of your Driving Test consists of oral questions on the Rules of the Road. When you are filling in the application form for a Provisional Driving Licence you are reminded that you should read the Rules of the Road carefully. Your signature is a declaration that you understand these rules.

You can get a copy of the Rules of the Road booklet from your nearest Motor Taxation office. Some Schools of Motoring stock them and if you cannot get a copy from one of these sources then you should write to the National Safety Council, 4 Northbrook Road, Ranelagh, Dublin 6. You should enclose sufficient stamps to cover the cost of postage.

While the number of questions asked is usually 5 or 6, it may be more and your answers should be accurate and reasonably detailed. It must be said, however, that you cannot fail the Driving Test by giving wrong answers. If, by your driving, you show that you know the Rules and how to apply them, then you will not fail on this score.

Here is a quiz to test your familiarity with the Rules of the Road. It is designed to get you thinking. Remember, though, it is not meant as a substitute for the Rules of the Road booklet.

1.   Here are 5 Road Warning Signs. Explain what each one means.

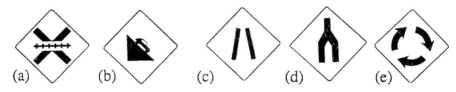

(a)   (b)   (c)   (d)   (e)

2.   What is the sequence of lights for motorists at a Pelican Crossing?
3.   Name three persons for whom you must stop.
4.   Where may you not park? {Several answers}
5.   What does a broken yellow line road marking signify?
6.   What signs mean NO ENTRY? {Two answers}
7.   When should you dip your headlights? {Seven answers}
8.   What should you do first in the event of an accident?
9.   What do the zig-zag markings at Zebra or Pelican crossing signify?
10.   When may you cross a continuous white line?
11.   Explain a broken white line near the edge of the road?
12.   When may you overtake on the left or inside? {Three answers}
13.   When may you overtake on the right?

14. Which traffic has right of way at a junction where the roads are of equal importance?
15. What does an amber traffic light signify?
16. What does a flashing amber traffic light signify?
17. What does a green traffic light signify?
18. How must you enter a roundabout?
19. What does a Clearway Sign indicate?
20. What do the following regulatory signs mean?

(a)   (b)   (c)   (d)   (e)

ANSWERS TO RULES OF THE ROAD 20 QUESTIONS QUIZ.

1   (a)   Unguarded level crossing.
    (b)   Steep descent ahead.
    (c)   Road narrows dangerously or narrow bridge ahead.
    (d)   End of dual carriageway.
    (e)   Roundabout ahead.

2. Green, Amber, Red, Flashing Amber, Green.

3. A Garda, a School Warden, persons in charge of animals, for pedestrians on various pedestrian crossings, flag-men on duty at roadworks or other obstructions.

4. You may not park in a prohibited area at or near a junction, on a corner, a bend or the brow of a hill, on a humpbacked bridge, double yellow lines, on a single yellow line, a clearway or bus lane during certain times, at traffic lights, pedestrian or pelican crossings, opposite a continuous white line or anywhere you could cause inconvenience or danger to other road users or pedestrians. You may not park more than 18 inches (45cms) from the kerb. Nor may you park wholly or partly on a footway.

5. A broken yellow line marks the edge of the carriageway. It indicates a "hard shoulder".

6. (a) A Regulatory Sign. Red circle, white background, black arrow pointing straight up with red bar through it.
    (b) A solid white line (nearest you) with a broken white line behind it across the width of the roadway.

7. You must dip your headlights when:
    (a) You meet other traffic.
    (b) You are closely following other traffic.
    (c) Within a well lit speed limit area.
    (d) Outside a speed limit area which is well lit.
    (e) At the beginning and end of lighting up time.
    (f) In dense fog or falling snow.
    (g) To avoid inconveniencing other traffic.

8. Stop your vehicle! Keep your vehicle at the scene of the accident for a reasonable length of time. (See Rules of the Road for further details).

9. You must not overtake another vehicle within the zig-zag markings. Nor may you park within that area. You may only stop within the marked area for traffic reasons such as yielding right of way to a pedestrian on the crossing.

10. You may cross a continuous white line if there is a broken white line to the left of it and it is safe for you to do so.

11. Broken white lines indicate the area in which parking is prohibited at a bus stop, taxi-rank or designated loading area.

12. You may *only* overtake on the left inside if:
    (a) The driver ahead of you has indicated right and you intend going straight ahead or left.
    (b) You have indicated your intention to turn left.
    (c) The traffic in the lane to your right is moving more slowly than the traffic in your lane.

13. You normally overtake on the right but you may only do this when it is safe and legal to do so.

14. Where roads are of equal importance you must yield to traffic coming from your right.

15. The amber light means stop, unless your vehicle is so close to the stop line that you cannot stop safely before crossing the line.

16. A flashing amber light means that you should yield to pedestrians who are on the crossing but proceed with caution if the crossing is clear.

17. Green means go, but you may only proceed if the junction or crossing is clear.

18. You must always enter a roundabout by turning left.

19. A Clearway Sign indicates that stopping or parking is prohibited (except for buses or taxis) during times shown on the plaque beneath the sign.

20. (a) Major road ahead. Give way to traffic approaching from either direction. Slow down and stop if necessary.
    (b) Clearway - restricted parking (see 19 above).
    (c) Appointed taxi stand - no parking for other vehicles.
    (d) No left turn.
    (e) End of speed limit area - maximum speed 55 m.p.h.

SCORING: When calculating your score you should allow yourself 5 marks for each question. In questions number 1 and number 20 you may have one mark for each sign you identify correctly. Remember that when you are on test you will not be asked as many questions as this. Nor will you be scoring out of 100 marks!

If your score is 85 - 100, this is excellent.
If your score is 55-85, this is fairly good.
If your score is less than 55, then you need to study the Rules of the Road booklet very closely.

REMEMBER: WHEN YOU APPLIED FOR YOUR PROVISIONAL LICENCE YOU INDICATED THAT YOU HAVE A SATISFACTORY KNOWLEDGE OF THE RULES OF THE ROAD

THE
ROAD TRAFFIC ACT AND YOU

All fines under the various Road Traffic Acts and their Amendments are imposed by the courts. Many people believe that traffic tickets placed on a vehicle or handed to a driver are on the spot fines. This is not so !

A Garda Síochána or a Traffic Warden will merely place a notice regarding an alleged offence on a vehicle. If the amount indicated on the ticket is paid to the Fines Office at Coleraine House Garda Station, Coleraine Street, Dublin 7, within 21 days, then no prosecution will follow. If the notice remains unpaid and the person is convicted of the offence alleged in the notice, a fine of up to £200 may be imposed.

There are thirteen types of offence which are covered by these traffic tickets.The notice will indicate the alleged offence and the amount payable.

The alleged offences and the amount payable for each are noted below.

£10 is levied for :

1. Standing a street service vehicle for hire at a place which is not an appointed stand.
2. Failing to bring an omnibus wholly within roadway markings at a stopping place or stand.
3. Parking a vehicle wholly or partly within roadway markings at an omnibus stopping place or stand.
4. Parking a vehicle in a place prohibited.
5. Parking a vehicle at a time prohibited.
6. Parking a vehicle for a time prohibited.
7. Parking a vehicle in a manner prohibited.
8. Parking a vehicle wholly or partly on a footway.
9. Parking a vehicle in a Meter Parking Place without paying the specified fee.
10. Parking a vehicle in a Disc Parking Place without displaying a valid parking disc.

£15 is levied for :

1. Parking a vehicle in a Bus Lane, with flow or contra-flow.
2. Stopping a vehicle on a clearway.

£50 is levied for:

1. Failing to display a current vehicle licence disc.

Places where parking is prohibited :
1. Within 5 metres of a junction.
2. At a continuous white line where there are less than 3 lanes.
3. At an appointed stand e.g. taxi rank unless your vehicle is a small public service vehicle.
4. Where you obstruct the entrance to a Fire Brigade or Ambulance station.
5. Where you will obstruct a vehicular entrance e.g. driveway except where you have permission from the occupier.
6. At a pedestrian crossing or within a pedestrian crossing complex.
7. At a loading bay.

The list of fines above relates specifically to Dublin Area Traffic Parking Bye-Laws 1986. Bye-laws may differ from area to area. Other fines which may be imposed cover other aspects of the Road Traffic Acts. Some of these are :

1. Driving a vehicle while under the influence of alcohol or drugs, where fines imposed may be as great as £1,000 and will usually include disqualification, endorsement of your licence, and possibly a term in prison.
2. Failure to wear a seatbelt can incur a penalty of up to £150. Another aspect of this is that Courts consider failure to wear a seatbelt as contributory negligence and will deduct about one fifth of any compensation awarded.
3. Failure to display a current insurance disc will also result in a heavy fine. At present on the spot fines are not used for this offence.
4. Careless driving and dangerous driving can also incur heavy penalties.

It is not possible to cover all offences under the Road Traffic Acts. But one final point worth mentioning is that a substantial fine and possibly a term of imprisonment may be imposed on a person found guilty of undergoing or attempting to undergo the driving test for someone else.

REMEMBER: OBSERVATION, ANTICIPATION AND CONCENTRATION ARE KEY ELEMENTS OF GOOD SAFE MOTORING!

ROAD SIGNS AND MARKINGS

There are many different road signs and markings which you may encounter as you are motoring. As previously mentioned, it is advisable to become familiar with these as they apply to the area in which your Driving Test will be carried out.

ROAD SIGNS

(A) **Warning Signs:** These are usually black paint on a yellow background. (see p.36).They are there to warn you that you are approaching a hazard or a potential hazard. Recently count-down markers have been introduced. They are white bars on a blue background and indicate an exit off a motorway. They are placed at intervals marking 300 metres, 200m and 100m from the exit.

(B) **Regulatory Signs:** These are usually a black arrow within a red circle on a white background, except for Yield Signs, Stop Signs and signs which mark the end of a speed limit area. You may, however, see regulatory signs which show a white arrow within a white circle, where the background is blue. They may be seen on pedestrian islands on a wide road. They dictate the direction traffic should go. Many roundabouts and dangerous bends now have fluorescent arrow markings to direct road users.

(C) **Information Signs:** These signs advise the road user. You may, for example, see a sign informing you that there is a "Roundabout ahead 200m" or "Cul de Sac". Information signs may also tell direction e.g. Waterford 14km. or give advance direction e.g. Limerick, Cork with an arrow showing the direction.

ROAD MARKINGS

Road markings are either yellow or white. Their function is similar to Regulatory Signs as they give orders.

(A) **Lines** (At the edge of the carriageway)
    1.Broken Yellow = Hard Shoulder or edge of the carriageway.
    2 Single Yellow = No Parking (times usually specified).
    3 Double Yellow = No Parking at any time. Stopping NOT allowed during Clearway times.
    4.Yellow Box Junction = Keep the junction clear. Do not stop on box unless exit road is clear.

(B) **White Lines** (Centre Lines)
    1. Broken White = Keep left unless it is safe to cross.
    2. Broken White (nearest you) with solid white line parallel =Keep left unless it is safe to cross.
    3. Broken White Lines parallel and joined with diagonals = Keep left unless it is safe to cross.
    4. Continuous White = Do not cross.
    5. Two parallel Continuous White = Do not cross.
    6. Continuous White (nearest you) with Broken White Parallel = Do not cross.

(C) **White Lines** (Across the carriageway)
1. Solid White = Stop line at traffic lights, crossings, Stop signs and Yield signs.
2. Solid White with Broken White behind it = No Entry.

(D) **White Markings** (Other than above)
1. Zig Zag Lines (At pedestrian lights and crossings) = No Parking; No overtaking;No stopping, except in traffic.
2. Buffer areas (at traffic islands etc.) = Avoid driving on marked area.
3. Hatched Junctions (See page 21) = Avoid overtaking if this means driving over markings.
4. Broken White lines: Marking traffic lanes on wide roads and roundabouts.
5. Words: Such as, No Entry;Taxi;Bus Lane;Loading Area etc.
6. Arrow Markings: Indicating lanes and traffic direction.
7. White Triangle: This means the same as a Yield sign.

As road traffic conditions are constantly changing and improving, road signs and markings are keeping pace. It is, however, worth noting that there is not always great consistency in the marking of roads from one area to another.

VEHICLE CHECK
DON'T ALLOW YOUR CAR TO FAIL YOUR TEST FOR YOU.
If you drive a defective vehicle, you are breaking the law. You may also represent a danger to other road users, to your tester and yourself. As part of the preliminaries to your test, you will have signed a statement that your vehicle is in a roadworthy condition.

So check the following:-
BRAKES, HANDBRAKE AND STEERING ADJUSTED PROPERLY.
WINDSCREENS CLEAN AND FREE FROM OBSTRUCTION, STICKERS ETC.
LIGHTS, REFLECTORS AND INDICATORS UNDAMAGED AND WORKING.
REAR VIEW MIRROR, HORN, SPEEDOMETER, WINDSCREEN WASHERS AND WIPERS. SAFETY BELTS.

CORRECT TYRES IN REASONABLE CONDITION AND AT CORRECT PRESSURE - You don't want to get a flat tyre on test. The writer is aware of one person whose test was cancelled because one of the windscreen wipers fell off when switched on as it began to rain, just as the test was complete. But for that, the applicant would have passed.

CONCLUSION

On the day of your test it will be all up to you! Your knowledge of the Rules of the Road, your practice and preparation and the instruction you have received will pay dividends. If you concentrate on good safe driving rather than the fact that you are on test, then there is no reason why you should not pass. Good Luck!

NOTES